"OMNIBUS TICKETS" IN LONDON

J C PURTON

EDITED BY
BRIAN PASK

The Transport Ticket Society
2000

Comments etc. regarding this publication are welcome;
please write to the Society's Publications Officer:

David Harman
24 Frankfield Rise
Tunbridge Wells
TN2 5LF

E-Mail: David.Harman@btinternet.com

ISBN 0 903209 45 4

Published by
The Transport Ticket Society
81 Pilgrims Way, Kemsing, Sevenoaks, TN15 6TD

Printed by
Paterson Printing Ltd,
Tunbridge Wells

Editor's Note

The first part of this publication consists of a three-part article by the late Jack Purton which originally appeared in Ticket and Fare Collection Society *Newsletter* in 1956 (pages 129, 143). The text of the original has been reproduced without alteration, apart from correction of one or two minor typing errors, but relevant illustrations (not practicable in 1956) have been added, together with footnotes giving appropriate references to the text. Thanks are due to Roger Atkinson and Graham Page for providing many of these illustrations.

The original article was followed up in T&FCS *Newsletter* by a number of comments from other collectors, and these constitute the second part of the publication. Again, the original text is unaltered, but relevant illustrations have been added and appropriate cross-references added in the original article.

Brian Pask
Ilford, Essex
September 2000

Contents

Part One – THE HORSE BUSES

Generally it is the practice of collectors to class all untitled "Omnibus Tickets" as printers' stock issues. However, in London for a period of about 30 years a very large number of such tickets, both of geographical and numbered stage varieties were in use. While they carried no operator's name, they were far from being "stock" tickets.

Among collectors who have specimens of these early issues there is a considerable amount of conjecture as to the use and ownership of such tickets. This has prompted the writer to try and throw a little light on the subject. Having no official information whatever, his only qualification is an interest in London tickets which has extended over his whole life, or at least since he was able to read at all, some 45 years ago. Any conclusions reached or statements made are the writer's own personal opinions and he would welcome other collector's ideas or corrections on the subject.

Tickets are said to have come into general use on the buses of the London General Omnibus Co. Ltd. in 1891, but it appears that geographical stage bell punch tickets may not have superseded the original roll type until 1893 [1]. From this time until at least 1910 London horse-buses almost always used the single-column named-stage ticket; that is a ticket with the operator's title and conditions set vertically along the right and left-hand edges, while the stage names were arrayed horizontally across the centre [2]. There were exceptions to this rule, but they do not affect our story, as the same remarks in general apply to the exceptions as to the single-column type.

Fig 1   Fig 2

[1] Apparently from 1st January 1893 - see page 15.

[2] This applied also to many motor buses later in this period. Typical tickets are illustrated from L.G.O.C. (Fig.1 - pink), British Automobile Development Co. (obviously motor bus - Fig.2 - white, green overprint), London Road Car Co. (Fig.3 - white, red overprint) and Thomas Tilling Ltd (Fig.4 - white, red overprint). Note that the method of showing the fare changed with time - fare in text only (Fig.1), fairly heavy overprint added (Figs.3/4) and thin overprint including word "FARE" replaced value in text (Fig.2).

Fig 3   Fig 4

While the majority of these tickets carried the operator's title, (at least, as far as the biggest operators are concerned), there were a fair number of horse-bus routes with tickets on which the operator's name did *not* appear. These tickets bore only the words, "OMNIBUS TICKET" where the title would usually be printed, although the full array of stage names would be carried.

The routes on which these tickets were in use were in almost all cases those controlled by the Associations of horse-bus operators common in London in the Nineteenth Century and which only finally expired in the years before the First World War. In passing, it may be mentioned that these Associations of bus owners are believed to have been in existence as early as 1832, only three years after George Shillibeer's introduction of his omnibus to the streets of London. Excessive competition led to the formation of Associations both to control existing proprietors on certain routes and to drive off or deter newcomers. (In this connection readers are advised to turn to Mr. J.M. Birch's articles on "Birches and Transport" in "Buses Illustrated" Nos.11 and 12).

Practically every operator of standing from the London General Omnibus Co. Ltd. with 1500 buses to Henry Pope and Sons with three was a member of one or more of these Associations. The only important exception was the London Road Car Co. Ltd., although this operator, towards the end of the horse-bus era, came to amicable working arrangements with them, without taking up membership.

The practice on horse-bus routes controlled by the Associations or at least on those routes controlled by the two largest, the Atlas and Waterloo Omnibus Association and the Camden Town Omnibus Association was for the owners of the buses to provide the bus and driver and for the Association to provide the conductor and tickets. The Association took the collected fare money at the end of the day and shared it among the various operators according to the number of buses they ran on the route. Among the smaller associations in which the London General Omnibus Co. Ltd. was by far the predominant partner, it was the practice for this company to provide the conductors and tickets and share out the takings [3].

On Association routes it was the custom to use "Omnibus Tickets" which were in 95% of cases exactly similar to the standard L.G.O.C. tickets of the period, even to carrying the identification number for the tickets of each route, according to the L.G.O.C. code [4]. (This number appeared at the left-hand bottom corner of each ticket in the case of single-column types, but in various positions in the centre in the case of the relatively few double-column type tickets. It seems to have been "For Official Use Only". The buses themselves did not display route numbers until 1909. The numbers then adopted were not the same as had been previously used on the tickets).

When the motor bus was finally ousting the horse-bus from its premier position (about 1909) the L.G.O.C. severed its connections with the Associations. This began a very confusing period on the horse bus routes that were left. A variety of "Omnibus Tickets" began to appear, mostly of the geographical type, often carrying the the the L.G.O.C. *official* route numbers which had been adopted by the big company from October 1908, onwards (*not* the former ticket code numbers). Obviously most of these tickets had no connection with the L.G.O.C., in some cases being by printers other than Bell Punch & Printing Co. Ltd. In such cases it seems that the remaining horse-bus operators or Associations had ordered their own tickets, basing them on the L.G.O.C. style previously used and in most cases copying the "Omnibus Ticket" titling, instead of using their own names as might have been expected [6].

Fig 5   Fig 6

Fig 7

Fig 8

In theory at least, the Atlas and Waterloo and the Camden Town Associations should have provided their own tickets, but in fact it appears that either the L.G.O.C. supplied them or that the Associations obtained them from the Bell Punch Company through the L.G.O.C. In the case of the smaller Associations it is almost certain that the L.G.O.C. supplied the tickets. These tickets would be in use on every Association bus on the route, no matter who owned it.

The only very minor exceptions to the L.G.O.C. being the supplier of tickets appear to be:-

(a) on one or two South East London routes where Thomas Tilling was the chief partner in the particular Association and the L.G.O.C. ran no buses. Even these tickets, though "full geographical" instead of "single-column named-stage" bore a code number in the *L.G.O.C.* series.

(b) on the Camberwell Green - Shoreditch route where there were some "full geographical" tickets with a Tilling code *letter*. (Tilling used these code letters on his own titled tickets on certain suburban routes which he operated independently). Why there should have been these "Omnibus Tickets" of obvious Tilling parentage, especially as L.G.O.C. titled *and* L.G.O.C.-style "Omnibus Tickets" also existed for the Camberwell Green - Shoreditch route, I am not sure [5].

Fig 9

Fig 10

Although the above remarks have been solely concerned with horse-bus tickets, it needs to be pointed out that similar

---

[3] For source of this information see page 12.

[4] Tickets from two of the Associations are illustrated - Kings Cross and Victoria Omnibus Association, showing LGOC code 28 (Fig.5) - white, red overprint) and Atlas and Waterloo Omnibus Association, code 71 (Fig.6 - white, purple overprint).

[5] For details of these Tilling style tickets see page 13; for background to changes on this route see page 15-16.

[6] Typical examples are shown at Figs.7 (yellow, purple overprint), 8 (white), 9 (yellow) and 10 (purple). Note route numbers 72, 82 and 88, also "AP" (see page 6) on Fig.8.

Fig 11

Fig 12

Fig 13

Fig 14

from the Kilburn terminus to Cricklewood (The Crown Hotel) on the same day. It is perhaps advisable to point out that Route 16 was not running under this number then; it did not receive it until October, 1908 [7]. It is however of interest to say that motor buses continue to run between Cricklewood The Crown and Victoria Station today over fifty years after they began to do so. In fact, the basic route 16 has been running between the same termini for a longer period than any other London service [8].

Fig 15

Fig 16

Returning to the tickets after this digression; on the forerunner of what became Route 1 an even more interesting position existed. Route 1, Cricklewood - Law Courts (later to Elephant & Castle) was pioneered by the London Motor Omnibus Co. Ltd. (the famous "Vanguard" concern) and was never a horse-bus route. It did, however, compete heavily with certain old-established horse-bus routes and to meet this competition the Atlas and Waterloo Omnibus Association arranged for its members to put motor buses on the Vanguard route. Most of these motors were owned by the L.G.O.C., but Messrs. Birch, Associated Omnibus Co. Ltd., Burtwell, Sharland and others also provided motor buses on which, as usual, named-stage horse-bus type tickets carrying in lieu of the operator's title, the words "Omnibus Ticket", were used. These Association buses were not sufficient to combat Vanguard and with the consent of the Association the L.G.O.C. put more motors on the route. On these extra buses the takings were not shared and tickets carrying the L.G.O.C. title were used. This meant that some L.G.O.C. motors were using L.G.O.C. titled tickets while others were issuing "Omnibus Tickets" on the same route [9].

Two other points regarding the horse-bus "Omnibus Tickets" require mention. Firstly, there were also numerical stage tickets of this type. They carried on the left stages 1 - 10 reading downwards and on the right 10 - 1 reading downwards, the columns being labelled "Up" and "Down" respectively. There were also plain "Omnibus Tickets", entirely without stage names or numbers, though with "Up" and "Down". Curiously, these carried an identification code number, 104 [10]. This may mean that the number code was

tickets were used on the early motor bus services where these were run by operators who were members of the Associations. Thus the earliest motor bus tickets of what is now London Transport Route 16 were "Omnibus Tickets". This was because the original horse route from Kilburn to Victoria Station had been worked by the Victoria Station Omnibus Association of which, among others, the L.G.O.C. Ltd., the Associated Omnibus Co. Ltd. and Messrs. Glover and T. Cane were members and had horse-buses working on the Kilburn route. When these operators placed motor buses on this road they were controlled by the Association and the same ticket methods prevailed. In fact, it is possible that Route 16 is unique in that horse and motor buses for a short period used exactly the same tickets, both types of vehicle running between the same terminal points and both being extended

---

[7] Four tickets from this route are shown; Fig.11 (white, purple overprint) original route to Kilburn; Fig.12 (lilac, purple overprint) extension to Cricklewood; Fig.13 (green, purple overprint) further stage "Garage" (all code 80); Fig.14 (white, purple overprint) route 16, LGOC title after withdrawal from Association.

[8] This may not be strictly true - for a time the Cricklewood terminal was the garage (Figs.13,14), later some buses ran to Wembley; by 1951 the terminus was Sudbury then (1993) Neasden or Brent Park and (2000) back to Cricklewood Garage.

[9] Two tickets from this route, both code 102, but "Omnibus Ticket" and LGOC titled respectively are illustrated at Figs.15 and 16 (both green, purple overprint).

[10] Examples of these numerical stage tickets are shown overleaf at Figs.17 (buff, purple overprint) and 18 (blue). Also, at Figs.19 (front) and 20 (back) is a white "Omnibus Ticket" from the last years of the horse bus, also without stage names or numbers but with an operator's advertisement on the back. (Compare with Fig.9)

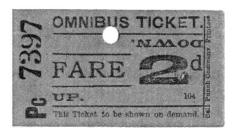

Fig 18

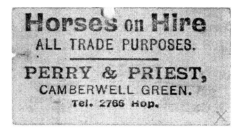

Fig 17   Fig 20   Fig 19

not purely a route number, but a combination route and ticket description code [11].

The second point concerns the "Omnibus Tickets" on the surviving horse buses of the 1909 - 1914 period, i.e. those which carried the official L.G.O.C. route number, now used on the buses themselves. On these the code number previously carried at the foot of the ticket disappeared and the mystic letters "AP" were shown. These were also shown on some L.G.O.C. titled tickets [12]. For some time I had been inclined to think that this might have stood for "Associated Proprietors", but Mr. H.J. Reinohl has put forward the suggestion that it means "All Prices" and I am now won over to this theory. "AP" would therefore mean that the same block was used for all values on that particular route. The best

evidence to support this is found in looking at the tickets which do not have "AP". For instance, I have some Route 24 [13], North Finchley - Ebury Bridge tickets of 1909, which carry the figures "1-8" at the foot of the centre column (signifying 1d to 8d?). Service 9, Bakers Arms - Turnham Green of similar type and date has two forms, 1d with "1" and 2d and 3d with "2 UP" at top-of centre column. (i.e. 1d and 2d and upwards?) Service 14, Putney - Boleyn Tavern, of similar type and date has "1-4" at foot, but to confuse the issue a 4½d of Service 3 has "O.P" at top of centre column and I can only suggest that this means "Odd Prices", perhaps for the odd-halfpenny values [14].

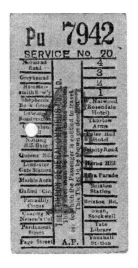

Fig 21   Fig 22   Fig 23   Fig 24

[11] See page 15 for details of these code numbers.

[12] A single column "Omnibus Ticket" from Services 91 & 92 is illustrated at Fig.21 and a two column LGOC issue from Service 20 at Fig.22 (both white, purple overprint).

[13] This must be an error; North Finchley - Ebury Bridge tickets were service 2 (see Fig.24).

[14] Examples of "2-Up" (Service 9) and "1-8" (Service 2) are illustrated at Figs.23 (pink, purple overprint) and 24 (orange, green overprint).

Part Two – THE PERIOD OF AGREEMENTS

The first phase of Omnibus Tickets had barely ended when a second one began. About 1913 [15] the London General Omnibus Co. Ltd. concluded a new agreement with Thomas Tilling Ltd. by which the maximum number of the latter concern's fleet was fixed and closer working arrangements made. This meant that L.G.O.C.Ltd. and Thomas Tilling Ltd. motor buses began to work in close co-operation on the same routes*.

* Note: There had been some joint workings before this time on a limited scale chiefly to meet National Steam Car Co. competition.

For a short period, both operators continued to use their own titled tickets, but very soon the L.G.O.Co.Ltd. seems to have become responsible for all tickets used on London routes worked by itself or by its associated operators. On routes worked solely by the L.G.O.C. and its other associated operators, tickets titled LONDON GENERAL OMNIBUS CO. LTD. were always used. However on *motorbus* routes on which Thomas Tilling Ltd. worked either jointly with the L.G.O.C. and/or their other associated operators, or entirely on their own, a completely new issue of tickets came into being. These always carried the words "OMNIBUS TICKET" and never the operator's title, though in all other respects they were standard L.G.O.C. geographical stage tickets of the period [16]. They were used on all the associated operators' buses on any route on which Thomas Tilling Ltd. buses

Fig 25   Fig 26

worked irrespective of the ownership of the buses. They were undoubtedly always ordered and supplied for use by the L.G.O.C.

It should, however, be pointed out that there was one exception to this rule. The National Steam Car Co. Ltd., which on 1st Jan. 1914 entered into a working agreement with the L.G.O.C. always used its own tickets (printed by Williamson of Ashton-under-Lyne) from the inception of the

Fig 27   Fig 28

company until it ceased London operations in November 1919. This applied even on routes such as that now known as L.T.E. Route 37, once shared by National and Tilling on which National used their own tickets and Tilling used the standard named stage "Omnibus Tickets" of L.G.O.C. pattern supplied by the L.G.O.C. [17].

I want to stress that the "Omnibus Tickets" were used only on routes on which Tilling buses worked and if for any reason

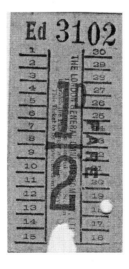

Fig 29   Fig 30

---

[15] For evidence for this date see page 13. For suggested earlier date see page 11.
[16] Examples are shown at Figs.25 (lilac, green overprint, c.1914) and 26 (blue, red overprint, c.1923).
[17] National and "OT" issues from Service 37 are shown at Figs.27 (yellow) and 28 (lilac, red overprint).

Fig 31

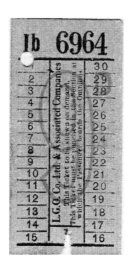

Fig 32

Tilling participation ceased the route reverted to tickets carrying the L.G.O.C. title. The reverse applied whenever Tilling buses commenced to work on a route on which titled L.G.O.C. tickets had been used. These were abandoned and a new "Omnibus Ticket" set was produced. Prior to 1914 a series of numerical stage tickets (stages 1 to 30) carrying the L.G.O.C. title was used by this company for new routes temporary shortages, etc. After the agreement with Tilling came into force this titled set was gradually used up and when new ones appeared they were all "Omnibus Tickets" of the familiar Bell Punch Co. 'stock' pattern [18]. It seems possible that the titled numerical stage issues were used up on purely L.G.O.C. routes while the new "Omnibus Tickets" were used where necessary on routes on which Tilling buses operated.

At some time in the early 1920's (probably about 1921/2) the policy was changed and completely new tickets began to appear titled "The London General Omnibus Co. Ltd. & Associated Companies" [19], either in full or abbreviated, according to space available [20]. These, geographical stage as usual, were first brought into use on routes on which Tilling shared operations but eventually superseded all other tickets on all routes whether previously using "Omnibus Tickets" or titled L.G.O.C. tickets. These new tickets were universally used on the buses of all the associated operators working in conjunction with, or controlled by, the L.G.O.C. and on the buses of the L.G.O.C. itself.

The foregoing remarks also apply to a new set of numerical stage tickets carrying the L.G.O.C. and Associated Cos. title [21] which eventually superseded the "Omnibus Ticket" set.

I must stress however that none of the above remarks apply to the outlying country routes worked on behalf of the L.G.O.C. by the National Omnibus & Transport Co. Ltd., The East Surrey Traction Co. Ltd., or the Thames Valley Traction Co. Ltd., who always used their own varieties of tickets on these routes. It may perhaps be helpful to say that as far as I know, none of the other L.G.O.C. associates such as British Automobile Traction Co. Ltd., Tramways (M.E.T.) Omnibus Co. Ltd., Associated Omnibus Co. Ltd., and so on, used anything other than standard titled L.G.O.C. tickets (or the later L.G.O.C. & Associated Cos. issue) after becoming associated with the big company, unless, of course, they worked on a route on which Tilling operated, in which case "Omnibus Tickets" were used.

[18] Examples of the LGOC and "Omnibus Ticket" sets of around 1914 are illustrated overleaf at Fig.29 (yellow, green overprint) and 30 (brick, green overprint). There seems to be some doubt whether the latter replaced the former immediately, and it seems more probable that both were in use together for a short period. The earliest "Omnibus Ticket" titled issues are in the style with solid overprints including the word "FARE", while tickets with both titles exist in the next style (said to date from 1915) with skeleton overprints without the word "FARE". Examples with LGOC title also exist with the red overprints introduced early in the First World War.

[19] See Fig.31 (white, red overprint).

[20] For more detail on this change see page 11.

[21] See Fig.32 (buff, red overprint).

Part Three – THE INDEPENDENTS

History repeated itself with the third phase of London "Omnibus Tickets" which were not stock tickets. While the process of changing on the combine vehicles to L.G.O.C. and Associated Cos. titled tickets was taking place the flood of post war independently owned buses was beginning. Most of these owners used either titled tickets or pure stock tickets.

Some half-dozen, however, used a peculiar type, unknown, I believe outside London. At first glance these appeared to be standard Bell Punch Co. Ltd. numerical stage 'stock' tickets with "Omnibus Ticket" and conditions in the centre column. A closer look, however, revealed small initials in a box at the foot of the centre column [22]. These initials in every case turned out to be those of either the owner or responsible official of the particular bus or buses using the tickets. A list of those known to exist may be useful:-

Initials		Fleet Name	
W.A.	William Allen	Premier	to L.P.T.B. 1933
R.N.	Robert Neal	Eclipse	to London Public O. Co.
R.T.	Robert Thackray	Rbt. Thackray	to London Public O. Co.
C.W.B.	Chas. William Batten	Atlas	to L.G.O.C.
H.W.B.	H.W. Batten	Britannia	to L.G.O.C.[23]

Fig 34

Fig 35

Fig 36

Fig 37

Fig 33

It seems possible this method of identifying the ownership of a ticket was cheaper than having a special titled set printed. Of these five operators all had sold out to larger operators by 1928 with the exception of Premier who had, however, by 1928

ceased to use this type of ticket except for emergencies, having by now a titled geographical stage set in use.

A somewhat similar type of ticket was also used in the last period of operation of one of the former London Tramway Companies, the Metropolitan Electric Tramways Co. Ltd. In this case, of course, the words "Omnibus Ticket" did not appear on the ticket. The centre column merely contained conditions that might have applied to any tramway company.

[22] Examples of these five sets of tickets are illustrated at Figs.33 (pink, red overprint), 34 (white, red overprint), 35 (green, red overprint), 36 (lilac, red overprint) and 37 (lemon, red overprint).

[23] There is clearly an error in this entry. The list of independents in "A History of London Transport" by Barker & Robbins, Vol.2, p.426-473 only mentions one Batten, the Charles William referred to in the previous entry. Also,

under Britannia Traction Co. Ltd., one of the proprietors is shown as William Henry Brown. So far as tickets are concerned, no example with initials "H.W.B." has been located, but examples are known with "W.H.B." (Fig.37), some with Britannia Motor Omnibus Service advertisement on the back. It thus appears that the first two columns of this entry should read "W.H.B." and "William Henry Brown" respectively.

The Company's title as such did not appear, just the initials MET were carried in a box at the foot of the centre column, while at the top was another box containing a letter, S,F, etc., as the case might be, which indicated the depot from which the conductor and/or car using the tickets worked. On a later style of these tickets these initials were very microscopic, in fact one needed quite reasonable eyesight to decipher them.

Reverting to independent London motor bus operators it may be of interest to recall that at one period many of these

Fig 38

operators were banded into Associations somewhat on the lines of the of the old horse bus associations, but much more loosely organised.

Thus the independent operators on the one-time 526D road between North Finchley and Wandsworth Bridge were all members of the West London Association of Omnibus Proprietors, which in turn was affiliated to the Association of London Omnibus Proprietors. This last body does not concern us as it was not an operating association, but really a kind of trade protection association for the independent London bus operators. The West London Association, however, of which Birch Brothers Ltd. were the leading members, was a controlling body on the 526D route. All buses of the various owners were painted in the red livery of the association and carried its "star" emblem as a fleet name. No attempt was made to pool takings and each operator continued to use his own tickets [24], titled or 'stock' as the case might be. The Association did issue a map and guide to the route it controlled and may have been unique among the London associations in doing so.

Other associations of the Independent era of 1922 - 1934 were a short-lived North London Association which combined operators working on what was to become route 284, Hadley Highstone to Victoria, and 285 Muswell Hill to Victoria, and was very loosely knit. There was a rather more important association in East London, the Eastern Omnibus Association, which controlled the many operators on route 511, Stratford to Chingford Mount on weekdays, extended to Chingford on Sundays. In both these last two associations there was no attempt to use a common livery or Association tickets. There was, however, in the case of the Eastern Omnibus Association a rather unusual set of Return tickets and possibly Exchanges which may have been issued by the Association. These carried on the front the name of the issuing operator, but on the reverse were the names of all the other operators on the route on whose buses the ticket was available for the return journey. The writer, in this case, is speaking purely from memory and would welcome any amplification regarding these tickets.

[24] A Birch Bros. fareboard issue from route 526d appears at Fig.38 (green, red overprint).

Resulting Correspondence

Query - Change in title on LGOC tickets

(This query and its answer were originally published in T&FCS Newsletter p.135/1960)

Query U

I have two London General Omnibus Co. Ltd. tickets of Service 73, a 7d and a 9d, which have a feature that, to me, is surprising. Both have on their fronts the title "LONDON GENERAL OMNIBUS CO. LD.", but on the backs "L.G.O.CO. LTD. & ASSOCIATED COS.". Mr. J.C. Purton in his article on pages 143 - 145, 1956, explained that the change to the "& Associated Cos." title was a gradual one that began early in the 'twenties. I had not, however, realised that it was so gradual as to affect one side of a ticket before the other. Can anyone explain whether this was an isolated phenomenon or a regular occurrence?

Answer U

This seemingly trivial question really plumbs historical depths of great interest. Mr. Purton on page 143, 1956 [25], explained that from about 1913/4 to about 1922/3 any route on which Thomas Tilling Ltd. ran had tickets in the normal L.G.O.C. "fareboard" design, but with "OMNIBUS TICKET" on the left, instead of any proprietor's title. Routes on which Tillings did not participate had L.G.O.C.-titled tickets.

Mr. A.W. McCall takes up the story:-

To begin with, I would date Tilling's motor bus use of "OMNIBUS TICKETS" from soon after the original sharing agreement of 6th May, 1909, rather than from the 1913 agreement, as I have a route 47 "OMNIBUS TICKET" in the style and colours of 1912. However, that is a side issue. From May, 1909 to May, 1915, the sharing of most routes on which Tilling participated was on a more or less equal basis, although there were one or two routes which, for convenience, Tilling operated exclusively. From 1915 to 1923 Tilling took over the entire operation of the previously shared routes. In 1923 a further agreement was made which enabled the Tilling company to double its London fleet. This led to Tilling participation in other routes, but these were shared and not exclusively Tilling operated. This meant that either these routes had to go back to the old practice of having "OMNIBUS TICKETS" for all buses, irrespective of whether Tilling or L.G.O.C. owned, or had to have separate L.G.O.C. and "OMNIBUS TICKET" sets. Neither course was adopted; instead the "L.G.O.CO. LTD. & ASSOCIATED COS." issues came into being.

The first tickets with this title may even have come in before the 1923 agreement, as I have one for Route 109 Forest Hill Stn - Chislehurst, which began on 12th April, 1922 and which was curtailed at Penge on 9th January, 1924.

At first the issues with the new inscription were confined to "shared" routes. It would seem, however, that soon the L.G.O.C. decided to extend the use of the new title to all tickets on all the routes it worked, but in order to avoid wasting printing plates, the Bell Punch Company was instructed to change the title only when an extension was made to the route concerned or the name of a fare stage was altered.

I possess the 7d and 9d tickets mentioned. The fare stage on Route 73a Roehampton Lane, Convent School on the L.G.O.C. print was changed to Roehampton Lane, Queen Mary's Hospital. As this stage change was on the back of the ticket, the new block for the reverse was given the new title, while the front block, which had undergone no change, kept the old title.

These route 73 tickets were not an isolated example; I possess similar examples from route 4 and 35.

As a matter of interest the last fresh set that I can trace to have been issued with the old L.G.O.C. title was that provided for the alteration of Route 93 to run between Harrow Weald and Wimbledon Station on 9th March, 1927 [26].

Fig 39

Mr. R. Atkinson has a theory:-

This is sticking my neck out with a vengeance, and I expect the usual penalty; but I have a theory - purely a theory - that the change from "OMNIBUS TICKETS" to the "& Associated Cos." tickets stems not from the 1923 agreement, but from another of March, 1922. (Tillings and L.G.O.C. seem to have loved making agreements). This March, 1922, agreement, (I learn from the Omnibus Society paper, "The London Omnibus Business of Thomas Tilling) laid down that the sharing was to be on the basis of tickets sold, as from 1st January 1922. I have no sound reasons to back up this theory, save that it would explain Mr. McCall's Route 109 ticket having the "& Associated Cos." title, even though the ticket should date right back to the inception of the route in April, 1922.

Mr. J.C. Purton comments:-

I have tickets from routes 15, 35 and 37 [27 - see footnote on following page]. with one title on the front and the other title on the back, but as far as I can remember, there were several more.

The surprising feature is not that these existed, but that no *bus* tickets ever seem to have existed with "L.P.T.B." on front and "L.G.O.CO.LTD. & ASSOCIATED COS." on the back

---

[25] Page 7 in this paper

[26] See Fig.39 (pink, red overprint).

Fig 40

Fig 41

Fig 42

Fig 43

Letter - Ordering of "Omnibus Tickets" by LGOC

(This letter and the resulting comments were originally published in T&FCS Newsletter p.158/1960)

"Omnibus Tickets' in London 1893-1927"

In the course of his article under this title on pages 129-131, 1956, Mr. Purton stated that the horse-bus Associations ordered their 'OMNIBUS TICKETS' through the London General Omnibus Co. Ltd [28]. If any proof of this is wished for, I think it can be found on the back of an 'OMNIBUS TICKET' that I have. It is route code 51, Ladbroke Grove (Lancaster or Earl Percy or Eagle) to Holborn Circus. It has on the back:-

> "This space to be let for advertising. For particulars apply to the Secretary, London General Omnibus Co. Ltd., 6, Finsbury Square."

C. Carter.

Mr. J.C. Purton comments:-

With regard to Mr. Carter. Am glad to hear of this ticket. I think my opinion of the L.G.O.C. ordering the tickets used by the Associations is a correct one.

As to my statement about fare-collecting practice on Association buses, (foot of page 129 and top page 130, 1956 [29]), I can quote Raymond W. Birch, whose paper on "London Bus Organisation in the 19th Century" was printed in the May, 1939 "Omnibus Magazine". Referring to the Associations Birch says:-

> "In those few* in which they (the L.G.O.C.) predominated, such as Bayswater (or 'John Bull') they took over the Association duties for the other proprietors, taking and sharing out all receipts. In the larger Associations, such as the 'Camden Town' and 'Atlas & Waterloo' the L.G.O.C. carried the Association's conductor and paid in and shared out like any other member."

* for "few" read "all except 'Atlas & Waterloo' and 'Camden Town Omnibus Association'" - *J.C.P.*

As far as Atlas & Waterloo tickets are concerned, on all A & W routes on which L.G.O.C. worked all my tickets are definitely of L.G.O.C. type and carry the code number. On the other hand on one or two A & W routes on which, to the best of my knowledge, L.G.O.C. did **not** work, such as Tulse Hill to Kings Cross (code 79) and Rye Lane to Victoria Station (code 78?) [30] the tickets **are** different, being double column in "full geographical" style, for example, first box "Tulse Hill to Camberwell Green" and so on, - reversed on other column [31].

However, the use of the code numbers even on these tickets raises the query, were the codes the L.G.O.C's. own or were they the Bell Punch Co's? Some of the Camden Town Association's tickets are non-standard, such as the 2d with "Going North" and "Going South" on the edges, but this may only have been because of the peculiar nature of the Camden Town routes in this instance. On the other hand, when the L.G.O.C. started to use **route** numbers these appeared on the 'OMNIBUS TICKETS' of both Camden Town and Atlas & Waterloo Associations in exactly the same style as on purely L.G.O.C. tickets [32]. The non-standard 'OMNIBUS TICKETS'

(or vice versa). Certain Effra Road **tram** tickets appeared with "L.P.T.B." on front and **Council's** conditions on the back, (i.e. L.C.C. conditions). This is mentioned by Mr. W.H. Bett at page 4 of the special publication, *"Some Notes on the 'Effra Road' Tickets of the L.C.C. Tramways and their Successors"*.

[27] Apart from the routes mentioned in the original article and above (4,15,35,37,73), such tickets also exist from route 42 and 65. An example from route 15 is illustrated at Fig.40 (front), Fig.41 (back) and one from route 37 (the reverse of that described earlier - it has LGOC & Associated Cos. title on the front; LGOC title on the back) at Fig.42 (front), 43 (back) (both tickets pink, red overprint).

[28] See page 4.

[29] Page 3 in this paper.

[30] This code was in fact 76. LGOC buses did work on both these routes - see page 15.

[31] A blue code 79 Tulse Hill - Kings Cross ticket of this type is illustrated at Fig.44. (overleaf)

[32] They also appeared on tickets of other associations - a Kings Cross & Victoria issue (by this time service 66) is shown overleaf at Fig.45 (white, green overprint) - compare with Fig.5 at page 4.

Fig 44

Fig 45

by other printers are all of the last days of horse-bus operation and all, or nearly all, carry the L.G.O.C. route numbers, although by this time the L.G.O.C. had ceased to be an Association member, or so I believe.

I mentioned in the Newsletter article a ticket from the Shoreditch - Camberwell Green route which carried a Thos. Tilling Ltd. route code **letter**. This is, in fact, not an 'OMNIBUS TICKET' at all, but is entirely without operator's title and carries no conditions of any sort. It is double column with "full geographical" stages in each direction, and code letter is K [33]. Very 'Tilling' in looks. I believe Tilling was chief operator on this route. Others L.G.O.C. and W.S. Jones & Sons.

None of this, of course, proves anything, but common sense points to L.G.O.C. having at least control of ticket design and probably ordering where they were concerned in route operation, though there is a possibility that both design and code numbering may have been controlled by Bell Punch Co. Ltd. themselves. This presupposes a high degree of organisation by B.P. Co. and a surprising lack of any personal whims on the part of the Associations.

Comment has also been invited from *Mr. A.W. McCall:-*

I feel that both Mr. Purton and Mr. Carter are right when they state that the horse-bus Associations ordered their 'OMNIBUS TICKETS' through the L.G.O.C., but Thomas Tilling Ltd. was a different proposition. Tillings issued their own titled tickets at least until the 1909 agreement referred to on page 136 last month, and I still think that Tillings were independent enough to have ordered their own tickets even when, after 1909, these had become 'OMNIBUS TICKETS', at least until the post-war era. (This, I realise, seems to conflict with Mr. Purton's view expressed on page 143, 1956 [34]).

[33] For explanation of use of Tilling style tickets on this route and illustration of ticket described see page 16.

[34] Page 7 in this paper.

Letter - Tilling and "Omnibus Tickets"

(This letter was originally published in T&FCS Newsletter p.181/1960)

Tilling and 'Omnibus Tickets'

Mac, of course, **may** be right about Tilling actually ordering the 'Omnibus Tickets' of the 1912-1922 period, (see pages 158/159, 1960 [35]); - but I doubt it. Not because I have any really concrete evidence in favour of my view, but simply because I have been studying the subject long enough to be generally able to arrive at the correct conclusions as far as London is concerned.

It is rather remarkable that if Tilling was responsible for the motor 'Omnibus Tickets', every development and change in L.G.O.C. ticket format took place in the 'Omnibus Tickets' step by step. I mean colour changes, overprint changes, type changes, etc. - and they did.

While I cannot prove anything at this late stage I think that if anything out of the ordinary had taken place on Tilling routes, I was quite observant enough as a youngster to have noted it. Nothing did, and I just automatically accepted from the earliest days that the 'Omnibus Tickets' were L.G.O.C. and never questioned, nor even heard the slightest whisper that they were Tillings' own tickets, which is quite remarkable, considering that I knew a lot of actual busmen in the 1913-1918 period and went to school with several busmen's sons. This may have been because we never suspected it, so the subject was never discussed.

A minor point that comes up is the 2d Cheap Midday Fare tickets of the first issue, - No.1, No.2, No.3 etc. (those grouping several routes on a ticket). Any ticket which covered a Tilling-worked route was automatically an 'Omnibus Ticket', which in this particular case must mean that either Tilling ordered tickets for L.G.O.C. routes, or here at least L.G.O.C. ordered 'O. T's [36]!

Again, I disagree that Tilling may have used the motor 'O.Ts.' from 1909, (see page 136, 1960 [37]). I had reasons for my date, "about 1913" on page 143, 1956 [38], as the commencing date for the use of 'O.Ts.':-

(1) Tilling first commenced to work on Route 36 when this route was diverted to Catford about the end of 1912. Tillings were quite a novelty in West Kilburn, (though not

Fig 46

Fig 47

[35] Page 13 in this paper.

[36] See Fig.46 - "No.1" LGOC title; Fig.47 - "No.2" "Omnibus Ticket" title (both blue, red overprint).

[37] Page 11 in this paper.

[38] Page 7 in this paper.

a greatly respected one), and I well remember that they used their own deaf and dumb tickets when they first came there. I cannot now remember for sure whether they were titled, but anyway, they were NOT L.G.O.C. tickets, and I am pretty sure that they were the standard motor bus Thos. Tilling Ltd. numericals of the period.

In the Omnibus Society's reprint of Klapper and Nicholson's paper, "Bus Services from London to the Country" it is stressed that L.G.O.C. did not come under Underground control till 1st January 1912. After mentioning subsequent agreements with B.A.T. Ltd. and Tillings, the article states:-

"First fruits of the new policy were apparent in June, 1912 when the Tilling Lewisham - Sidcup route became 39, Victoria Station - Sidcup. .... At the same time Route 36 ...... Liverpool St. - West Kilburn ..... was cut back to West Kilburn - Victoria, preparatory to extension to Catford". Well, I have two tickets of 39, Victoria - Sidcup, and they are both titled **L.G.O.C.**, (which I hope means that Tilling were still using their own, at least until new ones were printed) [39]. The extension of Route 36 came later, and initially, from my own observation, I know that Tillings used their own tickets on it, therefore, I said "about 1913" for the coming of the motor 'Omnibus Tickets'.

(2) My earliest, (at least in format) 'O.Ts' come from routes 10, 10 & 10A, and 35 & 35A. These are all of the type with the title running up the centre column and the service number between two lines thus:-

SERVICE 10

(Note there is no "No." between "Service" and "10"). I have never seen any earlier than this type. The use of 10**A** and 35**A** also dates them as 1912 or later [40].

I have, however, a "SERVICE **NO**.12" ticket, Turnham Green and Rye Lane, which was the first actual Tilling - L.G.O.C. joint route (to combat National). Klapper writes of it:-

"Made joint with Thos. Tilling on 8th May, 1911, to compete with National Steam Car Co. Ltd. as Turnham Green - Rye Lane, extended to Peckham Rye, October, 1911."

This is a pure L.G.O.C. ticket [41].

Going back to the subject of 'OMNIBUS TICKETS'. The Underground was responsible for all other printed matter that reached the public hands, - all publicity etc., so why not tickets? I never saw anything whatever in this connection that emanated from Tilling after 1913. Even the garages were built for them by the L.G.O.C.

Incidentally, as a sidelight on the somewhat exaggerated idea that is sometimes held of Tillings' general excellence and good name, I remember that they were regarded as a very rough old lot in Kilburn in pre-1914 days by the respectable inhabitants (and Kilburn then was lower middle and upper working class in character). Tillings men had a very tram-like uniform, - lined their pints up on the wall of the "Falcon". (Yes; this is literally true). And they had what we regarded as dingy old buses, - the petrol electrics.

Fig 48

Fig 49

Fig 50

Returning again to 'OMNIBUS TICKETS'; if they were bought by Tillings themselves, why not have Tillings' title and done with it? It seems to me that the only reason for 'OMNIBUS TICKETS' was either that L.G.O.C. did not wish to assume any legal responsibility by using their own title on tickets used on Tilling buses, or else Tilling jibbed at actually using L.G.O.C. - titled tickets.

J.C. Purton.

[39] An 8d from this route is illustrated at Fig.48 (brick, green overprint).

[40] A service 10 ticket of this type is illustrated at Fig.49 (yellow, green overprint). This style is generally dated as "c.1912", the previous type (with "Service No..." at the top) being dated as "c.11/1911".

[41] A 6d from this route is illustrated at Fig.50 (orange, green overprint).

Letter - Codes on LGOC tickets

(This letter was originally published in T&FCS Newsletter p.159/1961)

Codes on L.G.O.C. Horse Bus Tickets

My August, 1960 Newsletter arrived after I had left for Australia; hence the delay in writing to you. I am pleased that there is still some interest in London General and Associated Companies' horse bus tickets.

On page 158, 1960 [42], the correct code number for the Rye Lane - Victoria route is 76, and five London General omnibuses **did** work on this route, being subsequently lettered, TK-A to TK-E. I went to school near Victoria Station and frequently saw buses on this route.

Code 78 was the Paxton Hotel, Gipsy Hill and Brixton route, an association on which Star Omnibus Co. (London) Ltd. buses worked, but no L.G.O.C.

London General published a list of routes, under date 3rd April, 1899, on which their buses worked. They list 1923 buses on 81 routes, including 'Break' buses. Under the Route Tulse Hill - Kings Cross, Code 79, they list one bus, which would indicate that at one time at least one L.G.O. worked on this route, though I never saw it.

On the point regarding who inaugurated the code numbers, the L.G.O.C. or the Bell Punch Company. When I visited the late Mr. Noakes at Chiswick Ticket office, he showed me a large book in which the L.G.O.C. had pasted printer's proofs of their tickets printed by Bell Punch. An introductory note stated that all tickets would be printed as from 1st January, 1893, and the pages were headed from Index 1 to Index 127, which would indicate that the small index number, or code number, originated with the L.G.O.C., rather than with Bell Punch. The index number was printed in small figures on each ticket.

A complete range of tickets was preserved up to index 90. From that number on, only one 1d ticket was kept for each route up to index 127. Of the 127 index numbers there was no ticket preserved for index 83, nor 119 to 126 inclusive. However, I do myself have tickets bearing the index numbers, 120 to 126A. Index 127 commenced 27th October, 1908 and five days later became service 50. Indices 107 to 127 are dated after 1905, several of these being motorbus routes [43].

Tickets prior to index 91 have a note of the date when a change was made, such as index 12, Bow Bridge - Oxford Circus, 1/1/03 to Notting Hill Gate, another change 28/9/03 and still another 1/10/05. Such changes would occur when fares were reduced and more stage names added to the ticket.

From this book, it would appear that the L.G.O.C. ordered tickets where Associations were involved, (as, indeed, was demonstrated on page 158, 1960 [44]). Under index 9, Clapton - Elephant, a note indicates "made OT 8/9/02", - this could have been the date when Thomas Tilling Ltd. ran buses on this route in association with the L.G.O.C. (OT presumed to represent "OMNIBUS TICKET" *Ed. R.A.*)

There were two distinct types of ticket printed; one being where the stage names were printed one under the other, which has been referred to as the 'menu' type, (also as 'Teddy Bear's Picnic - see p.87, 1961. Ed.), and the other where the fare stages appeared in two columns, one column being the reverse way. I usually refer to this type as 'sides'. Each type is known with both L.G.O.C. title and "OMNIBUS TICKET" title.

Fig 51

Fig 52

Fig 53

Fig 54

When service numbers were used on all London General omnibuses, and those associated through the various Associations, on 1st November, 1908, new tickets appeared with the heading "SERVICE NO. " in bold print, and the small code number eliminated. The service number also appeared on each vehicle. Motor bus routes were originally allocated the first 30 numbers, with the horse buses taking 31 to 92, and when a new route started shortly afterwards it became service 93, the highest service number on a horse bus route. The London Motor Omnibus Co. Ltd. ("Vanguard") had started service numbers shortly after their commencement in 1905, and the L.G.O.C. adopted them following the amalgamation of July, 1908.

Regarding Mr. Purton's ticket with code K [45]. Shoreditch Church - Camberwell Green was code 16 and became Service 55 on 1st November, 1908, and the L.G.O.C. horse buses were withdrawn two years later, leaving Tillings,

---

[42] Page 12 in this paper.

[43] There were also some "a" suffixed numbers as well as numbers with an "s" suffix, the latter used when a ticket covered part only of a long route (comparable with the "X" route number suffixes used in later years). The "s" suffix tickets carried a vertical or diagonal red line overprint as on the code 21s issue at Fig.51 (white, red overprint)

[44] Two LGOC issues from this route are shown at Figs.52 (white, purple overprint) and 53 (green - note bus/tram booking to Epping Forest); later "OT" issue at Fig.54 (white, purple overprint).

[45] See pages 4 and 13.

Fig 55

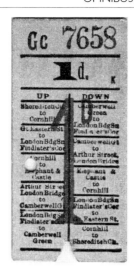

Fig 56

James Lavell and W.S. Jones & Sons as the Association. Tilling-type tickets then came into use bearing the title, Route "K" [46]. The same applied when the L.G.O.C. were withdrawn from Service 35, Finsbury Park - Clapton in December, 1910, leaving Tillings to operate this route. The new Tilling tickets were headed, Route "O". Tillings used code letters on their tickets similarly to the London Road Car Co. Ltd., but the latter company used the same letters as route letters on both side panels of their vehicles.

Following the withdrawal of L.G.O.C. horse buses, Service numbers continued to appear on some Association tickets, some being printed by Williamson [47].

H.J. Reinohl.

[46] A code 16 "Omnibus Ticket" is shown at Fig.55 (salmon, purple overprint) and a Tilling style code "K" issue at Fig.56 (white, green overprint).

[47] See page 4.

Other Publications

London Transport Numerical Stage Punch Tickets - Bob Williamson
    Checklists of all known "deaf and dumb" type punch tickets from 1933 onwards.

Part 1 - Tram and Trolleybus	£3.50
Part 2 - Central Buses	£3.50
Part 3 - Country Buses and Green Line Coaches	£2.50
Part 4 - Prepaids	£3.50
Part 5 - Miscellaneous	£3.50

London in 1997 - Brian Pask
    Comprehensive survey of tickets and ticket systems in the Capital, covering bus, tube, rail and river services.   £2.50

INTIS - Brian Boddy
    The British Rail Intermediate Ticket Issuing System: a comprehensive guide in two volumes. (*)   £8.00

Greater Manchester in 1998/9 - Paul J Smith and Brian Hughes
    Complete survey of tickets and ticket systems, covering bus, tram and rail. (*)   £4.50

The Tickets of the Grimsby & Immingham Electric Railway - Brian Pask
    All known tickets described, with numerous illustrations, faretables and map. (*)   £4.75

The Tickets of Hants & Dorset Motor Services 1920-1987 - Part 1 - Punch Tickets - Andrew Waller
    Exhaustive history detailing all known punch tickets. Fully-illustrated with tickets, faretables and two maps. (*)   £5.50

South Yorkshire Supertram - Fares and Ticketing - 1994-1997 - Dave Aspinwall
    A compilation of tables and diagrams, detailing fares, tickets and machine validations. Fully illustrated. (*)   £5.50

Tickets of the West Midlands PTE Part 4 - 1983-1986 - Robin Oliver
    Details of all known tickets issued in the final years of the PTE as a bus operator. Fully illustrated.   £5.00

* including illustrations in colour

All prices include postage and packing. Order from the Publication Sales Officer:

Steve Skeavington [X]
6 Breckbank,
Forest Town,
Mansfield,
NG19 0PZ

 **The Transport Ticket Society**

..... offers something for everyone interested in the study and collection of transport tickets, whether casual collector or serious student:

- Monthly, illustrated *Journal* with ticket news from the UK and around the world, articles on tickets, both historical and present-day, and much more.
- Regular distributions of obsolete transport tickets from the UK and overseas.
- Ticket exchange pools, circuits and postal auctions.
- Publications on tickets and related topics.
- Extensive library of ticket and transport items.
- Regular meetings in London, Manchester and Birmingham.

For a *FREE* sample Journal and membership details, send two first-class stamps to the Membership Secretary:

Courtney Haydon [X]
4 Gladridge Close
Earley, Reading
RG6 7DL

E-Mail: courtney@gladridgecl.demon.co.uk

http://www.btinternet.com/~transport.ticket